Cheers!

CELEBRATING ONTARIO WINES AND LOCAL FLAVOURS

Published in 2010 by
Binea Press, Inc.
512-1673 Richmond Street
London, Ontario, Canada N6G 2N3

Tel: 519.660.6424
Fax: 519.660.4449

E-mail: bineapress@bellnet.ca
www.bineapress.com

Distributed by:

Binea Press Inc.
519.660.6424

Library and Archives Canada Cataloguing in Publication

Bain, Richard (Richard G.), 1954-

Cheers! : Celebrating Ontario Wines and Local Flavours

Richard Bain; Foreword by Jim Cuddy

ISBN 978-0-9812993-6-5

1. Wineries – Ontario – Pictorial works. 2. Wine and wine making – Ontario – Pictorial works.
3. Vineyards – Ontario – Pictorial works. 4. Ontario – Social life and customs – 21st century – Pictorial works.
I. Title.

TP559.C3B34 2010   641.2' 209713   C2010-905960-3

14 13 12 11 10   1 2 3 4 5

Copyright © 2010 by Binea Press, Inc.

Design by Amanda Jean Bolte
Pazzo Creative
London, Ontario, Canada
Tel: 519.660.6424

Printed in Canada by Friesens Corporation
Altona, Manitoba

CELEBRATING ONTARIO WINES AND LOCAL FLAVOURS

RICHARD BAIN

FOREWORD BY
JIM CUDDY

For Donald Ziraldo

Rosehall Run Vineyards winemaker Dan Sullivan toasts the terroir with a glass of Chardonnay at his winery in Prince Edward County. Terroir is a French term applied to the characteristics of a region that give a specific personality to wine.

FOREWORD

It was a particularly beautiful hot July day and I was barrelling down the QEW with my bike in tow to do some Niagara wine-country research. What could be better? Cruise along country lanes by the vineyards, take a few notes, lunch and then see my old friend Barney Bentall perform at the Old Winery that night. The summer had been a hot one with early rain, so all the fruit was well ahead of schedule and the fields were a beehive of activity.

I parked at the Old Winery and hopped on my bike to head through Niagara-on-the-Lake. The first thing you notice is the number of tourists. The streets were full of families, couples and cyclists like me and it was only midweek.

It is a good distance to the wineries so I was blissing out along Niagara River Parkway, enjoying the sun. I had been along here many times but had somehow overlooked the magnificent view of the mighty Niagara River through the tree-lined banks. Across the road were homes with big manicured lawns and huge old graceful shade trees. The colonial mansion of Peller Estates came into view. Wow! It was set back from the road with vineyards in the front and the fields were full of straw-hatted workers culling the vines. It was quite a sight. As I pulled in, I had to navigate through hundreds of excited folks waiting for tours or having their pictures taken in front of the winery. Apparently the secret was out. When had this happened? When had our funny-looking little sister turned into such a beautiful woman? I was obviously not the most observant wine lover in Ontario.

Farther along the parkway there were more surprises: the Frank Lloyd Wright-inspired architecture of Lailey Wines, the broad-beamed elegance of Inniskillin and the simple farmhouse charm of Cattail Creek. There was an amazing array of styles and imagination and beauty along the road.

I pulled over to a fruit stand to take stock and scribble some notes. I bought a peach and as precious as this might sound, it was the greatest, most succulent peach I had ever tasted. I was truly stunned. Was this what Karl Kaiser and Donald Ziraldo had in mind 35 years ago when they foolishly thought they could grow the world's most renowned grapes in the shallow limestone of Southern Ontario? When Donald was pushing his wines on the steakhouses of Toronto, where the bluebloods dined, did he really believe he would succeed? Brave men. There was now ample evidence to support their vision, but there must have been some dark days. They correctly assessed the effect of the mighty and temperate Lake Ontario and the protection given by the escarpment from Beamsville along the "Bench" to Niagara. Good on them. But I think it was also that they saw a paradise no one else did and knew it needed to be preserved and shared.

Similarities abound between Niagara and Prince Edward County, where I spent a great deal of time as a boy. My grandfather had a dairy farm there and when I was growing up I spent my summers on his farm. One time walking "back the lane" with my grandfather, two things occurred that I have never forgotten. One, my grandfather took out his upper teeth to clean some wheat seeds from them. At the time I didn't know that was anatomically possible. Two, he told me the small farmers of the area never had a chance. "Unless you grow fruit you will never make it here. Farms are too small, too rocky and there are too many acts of God working against you." It scared me to think that the farm I loved so much might not always be around.

Prince Edward County was an area of many assets and many liabilities. There was fresh water everywhere – little lakes, streams and all the land along the shoreline of Lake Ontario. There were orchards and beautiful fields and tidy little towns strung together by winding county roads. But the land was rocky and the winters were harsh and there were those acts of God to watch out for.

Today, Picton, the hub of Prince Edward County, is unrecognizable from my early days of walking down Main Street to go to a matinée at The Regent Theatre. There are fine food stores, B & Bs, gelato parlours and your choice of many splendid restaurants. How did this happen? Wineries, plain and simple.

With the magnificent Peller Estates Winery in the background, a couple enjoys the fruits of the Niagara region's wine industry.

One of Niagara's most cleverly designed barrel cellars is at Malivoire Wine Company along the Beamsville Bench. Its "living roof" contributes to a near-perfect year-round temperature. Malivoire takes an innovative and eco-centric approach to winemaking that includes Niagara's first gravity flow production facility.

Back in the late '90s, a few reckless pioneers looked at the land near the lake. They saw the same mixture of clay and shallow limestone that worked so well for growing grapes in Niagara. Here was an area that also grew amazing fruit but had a harsher winter. Undaunted by the labour-intensive practice of covering the roots of the vines every winter to keep them from freezing, wineries such as Closson Chase and Long Dog began to grow grapes. No pioneer experience would be complete without an act of God or two to knock you down a peg. One deadly cold winter and in the spring you were replanting your vines. But somehow they prevailed and a new culture grew up around Prince Edward County.

The longtime residents of Prince Edward County always knew there was a beautiful, gently beating heart in the area. It was the body that needed a little work. Now Prince Edward County is full of tourists coming to visit the wineries, taste the wine and luxuriate in the countryside. Many city folk have been lured to the area to buy old farmhouses and cottages. Prince Edward County is looked upon as a treasure to nurture and preserve. With more than 30 wineries and cider and cheese makers in the locale, the county is looking very pretty indeed. So my grandfather was right and wrong. The small farmer did have trouble surviving, but thanks to the foresight and perseverance of some brave mavericks, the county has been reborn. Thank heaven for small miracles.

We are truly blessed in Ontario. I still must explore, hopefully by bike, the dusty backroads of Pelee Island and the sun-drenched north shore of Lake Erie. Here, among sandy shorelines and abundant wildlife, vintners continue family traditions, working the land, tending to their vineyards, surrounded not only by vines bearing grapes, but also by fruits and vegetables in this remarkably fertile soil.

As I pedalled back to the Old Winery after many hours of meandering through the timeless countryside, I felt strangely satisfied. This was my province, my backyard and somehow we all shared the stewardship of this immense beauty.

Jim Cuddy

The majestic Kitchen House, built in 1885, is a classic Queen Anne revival Victorian manor. It overlooks the vineyards at Peninsula Ridge Estates Winery, as well as Lake Ontario and the Toronto skyline.

I've been travelling the highways and biways of Ontario's wine routes for over 20 years, and I can say without a doubt there's real passion and excitement from both winemakers and consumers alike. From the winemakers it's because they get to work with a different and challenging vintage every year; and the consumers are discovering great, world-class wines are being made in their own backyard.

Michael Pinkus - Grape Guy
Wine Writer, Broadcaster and Educator

ABOVE: Visitors enjoy lunch at The VIEW Restaurant at EastDell Estates Winery.

LEFT: The Heron's Nest Cabin at EastDell Estates Winery is a great rustic getaway nestled in the vineyard on the Beamsville Bench.

ABOVE: Canadian wine industry pioneer Paul Bosc has two passions — the award-winning wines produced at the Paul Bosc Estate Vineyard and his Egyptian Arabian horses. Here he leads El Moor, also known as Eddie, who was born on the estate. Equuleus, the flagship red wine of Bosc's Chateau des Charmes, is named in honour of the horses.

RIGHT: Niagara Helicopter tours give sightseeing passengers an up-close view of the vineyards at Chateau des Charmes winery.

The wineries of Prince Edward County encourage one to savour, linger and enjoy. They are an enterprise that adds another unique dimension to the dynamic economy of the county, a pillar of the region's agriculture, an innovation in local industry, a delight for visitors. The county's wineries epitomize the simplicity and luxury of life on this island.

*Lawrie J. Ackerman, General Manager
Prince Edward County Chamber
of Tourism and Commerce*

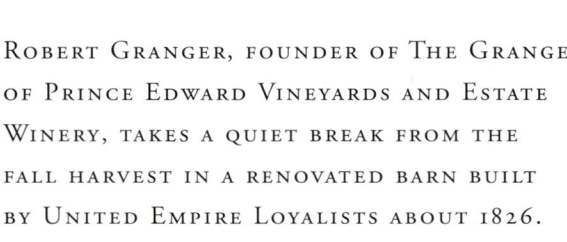

Robert Granger, founder of The Grange of Prince Edward Vineyards and Estate Winery, takes a quiet break from the fall harvest in a renovated barn built by United Empire Loyalists about 1826.

The wines in the vintner's cellar at Cave Spring Cellars in the village of Jordan are blessed by Bacchus, the Greek god of wine.

The entrance to the Cave Spring cellar is through the old bottle cistern, circa 1830s, and past a grape press that has been in the Pennachetti family, proprietors of Cave Springs, for more than 50 years.

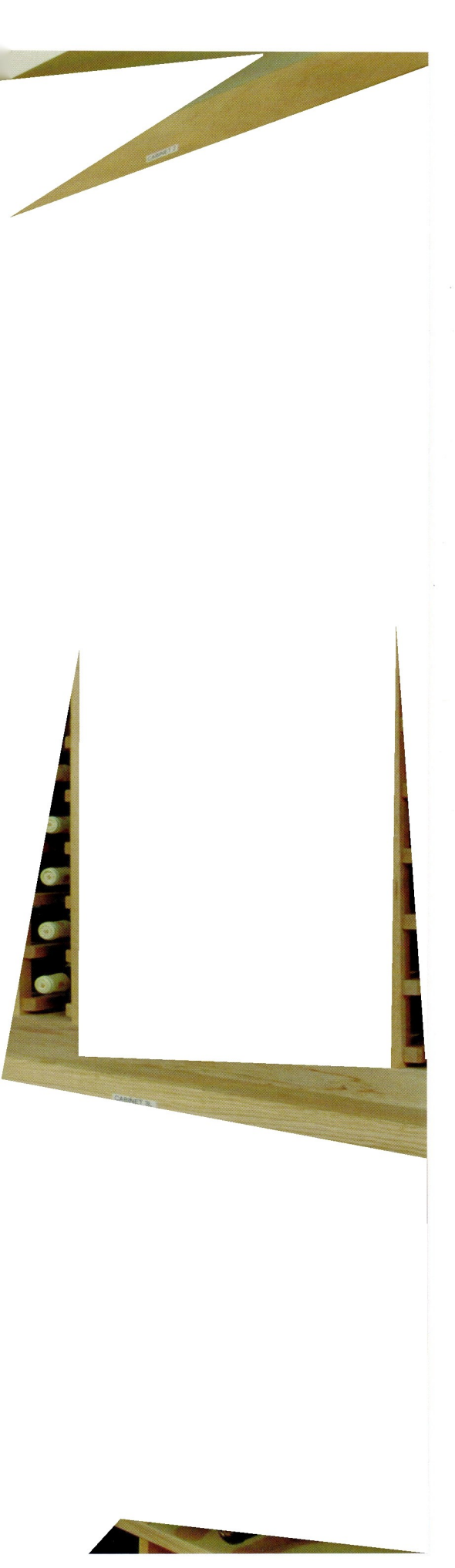

ABOVE: DR. DARYL SOMERS, RESEARCH DIRECTOR OF APPLIED GENOMICS AT THE VINELAND RESEARCH AND INNOVATION CENTRE, INSPECTS A DWARF PINOT MEUNIER PLANT. RESEARCHERS EXPLOIT THE RAPID CYCLING NATURE OF THIS DWARF GRAPE FOR ACCELERATED BREEDING PURPOSES TO HELP THEM IDENTIFY NEW AND DESIRABLE GENETIC TRAITS.

LEFT: THE FAIRMONT HOTELS AND RESORTS WINE CELLAR, ONE OF THE LARGEST IN CANADA WITH A 43,000-BOTTLE CAPACITY, IS LOCATED IN THE COOL CLIMATE OENOLOGY AND VITICULTURE INSTITUTE AT BROCK UNIVERSITY IN ST. CATHARINES.

Students in the Canadian Food and Wine Institute program at Niagara College in Niagara-on-the-Lake taste a variety of vintages in the wine-tasting theatre.

Salad ingredients await their fate in the cold food production lab at the Canadian Wine and Food Institute, the umbrella for the culinary, wine and beer education programs at Niagara College. The programs serve students, employers and consumers.

Mike Weir may be best known to the world as a golfer and Masters Champion but since he founded Mike Weir Wines in 2005, his name is also becoming synonymous with fine wine. At the Champions Dinner in 2004 after his Masters win, he insisted that the wine served be VQA wine from Niagara. Proceeds from the sale of his wine go to the Mike Weir Foundation, helping children with physical, emotional and financial needs.

Customers enjoy the tasting bar at Wayne Gretzky Estate Winery in Vineland, a popular destination for fans of both wine and hockey.

Angels Gate Winery nestles against the Niagara Escarpment and serves as a backdrop for the Pinot Noir vineyard at Rosewood Estates Winery along the Beamsville Bench. Angels Gate was founded by a group of wine-loving friends on a property once owned by the Congregation of Missionary Sisters of Christian Charity in Ontario. In 1995, the land was converted into a vineyard.

A sedge-hatted worker cultivates the vineyard at Angels Gate Winery.

upper: The fruit of the vine is bottled at Mastronardi Estate Winery in Essex County, along the north shore of Lake Erie.

lower: Employees at Stratus Vineyards in Niagara-on-the-Lake work at the fruit-sorting table during harvest.

Fermentation tanks gleam at Fielding Estate Winery along the Beamsville Bench, while visitors in the background sample wines in the Wine Lodge. The lodge pays tribute to Northern Ontario's cottage country, with cedar, stone, glass and a stunning view of Lake Ontario.

Juice trickles from the hydrologic basket press in preparation for making icewine at Pillitteri Estate Winery in Niagara-on-the-Lake.

With hopes for a great vintage, Inniskillin winemaker Bruce Nicholson watches the Cabernet Franc being emptied into the loading hopper in late autumn.

A starling manages to harvest an icewine grape at Inniskillin in Niagara.

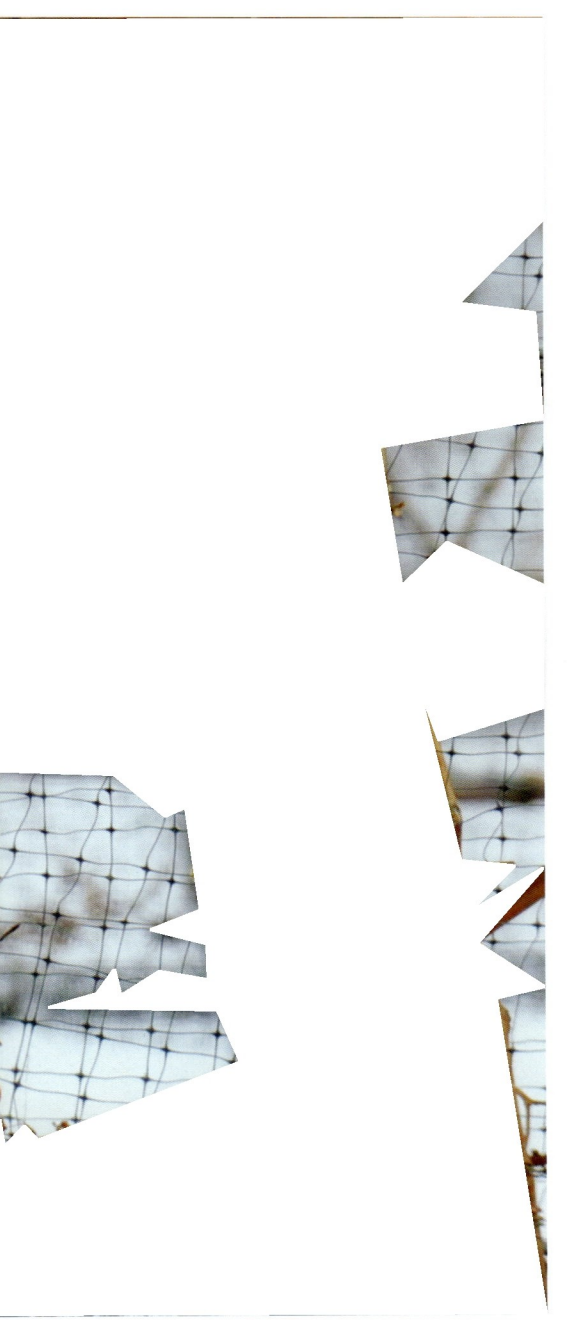

A basket of hand-picked icewine grapes awaits pickup at Inniskillin.

A flock of startled starlings retreats from a vineyard along the Niagara Parkway.

The remarkable improvement in Ontario wines over the past quarter-century can be attributed, without a doubt, to a firm determination on the part of our vintners to excel, hard work and the willingness to take chances in a time of uncertainty. Consumers in this province, who many years ago chose Ontario wines out of loyalty and patriotism, now do so because they are simply among the very best in the world, a fact confirmed by their outstanding success in international competitions.

Jim Bradley, MPP, St. Catharines

Ice bars, roasted chestnuts and hearty taste sensations are served up at the Niagara Icewine Festival, held each January in Niagara-on-the-Lake.

39

ABOVE: Friends enjoy the casual fine dining and selection of VQA wines at Inn on the Twenty in the village of Jordan.

RIGHT: Visitors linger at lunch under the pergola of the historic William Woodruff House at Ravine Vineyard in St. Davids. The pergola is the original post and beam shell from the homestead, built about 1827.

ABOVE: Students in the bake lab at the Niagara-on-the-Lake campus of Niagara College produce a variety of appetizing delicacies. The college offers certificate, diploma and apprenticeship programs that will lead its graduates to careers in the culinary, wine and beer industries.

LEFT: Canadian Wine and Food Institute Chef Professor Michael Olson and his wife, college booster Anna Olson, check out a bottle at Niagara College. Anna is co-chair of the Capital Campaign for Campus Improvements.

The impressive entrance to Southbrook Vineyards in Niagara-on-the-Lake is set between two large ponds filled with river rock. The winery's harmonious relationship to the land is expressed in each part of its operation.

Tarts and sour cherry preserves are among the temptations in the Bakery Café and Market at 13th Street Winery on 4th Avenue in St. Catharines.

The works of notable Canadian artists are showcased in the Gallery Room at 13th Street Winery. These art and wine lovers study paintings by featured artist Daniel Solomon.

Visitors come to Niagara for many different reasons and obviously have millions of different experiences. But those who are drawn here for the wine experience – the tasting, the touring, the learning and the appreciation of the amazing wines created from grapes grown right where they can see them – those are the visitors that truly feel a connection to Niagara and return during all seasons. From icewine in early winter through to harvest in the late fall, it's a cycle that affords lots of opportunities for remarkable visits.

*Janice Thompson
Executive Director
Niagara-on the-Lake Chamber of Commerce*

THE PRINCE OF WALES HOTEL IN NIAGARA-ON-THE-LAKE, BUILT IN 1864, IS A FAVOURITE GETAWAY DESTINATION FOR TOURISTS EXPLORING NIAGARA WINE COUNTRY.

Located in the sub-appellation of Twenty Mile Bench is Tawse Winery, which produces wines using organic and biodynamic practices. Its single-vineyard bottlings are a true expression of the Niagara terroir that surrounds the winery.

Local grapes, a commitment to quality – to me VQA represents a foundation for our talented winemakers to craft authentic wines that are a true reflection of the wine regions of Ontario. Origin and quality are inexorably linked and VQA speaks to the vital tie to the earth and nature that rules every wine and inspires the passion and ingenuity of every winemaker.

Laurie Macdonald, VQA Ontario

ABOVE: A worker sorts Sovereign Coronation grapes at Reif Estate Winery for its Niagara Raisins. The grapes are dried in refurbished tobacco kilns.

LEFT: Bottles of Rosé from Oak Heights Estate Winery, a craft winery in Warkworth, await sampling at the Taste Festival in Prince Edward County.

Generations of Ontario grape growers and winemakers have created a world-class industry and tourist destination, making this region the undisputed wine capital of Canada. Each one of us can now enjoy this legacy and with every taste savour what the good earth and skilled hands have made available to us.

Patrick Gedge, President & Chief Executive Officer
Winery & Grower Alliance of Ontario

ABOVE: DINERS ENJOY LUNCH AND A GLASS OF WINE ON THE SUNNY PATIO OF THE HILLEBRAND WINERY RESTAURANT.

LEFT: LOCALLY INSPIRED DISHES ARE FEATURED AT THE WINEMAKER'S LOOKOUT RESTAURANT AT HILLEBRAND ESTATES WINERY IN NIAGARA-ON-THE-LAKE.

AWAITS VISITORS AND LOCALS AT THE STONE ROAD GRILLE IN NIAGARA-ON-THE-LAKE.

Bocci, the vineyard dog, keeps an eye on the harvest at Featherstone Estate Winery in the Twenty Mile Bench sub-appellation of the Niagara Escarpment.

Wine tasting journals lean on an old rusty piece of tin roof sporting the No. 30 wine club name at Thirty Bench Wine Makers in Beamsville.

At Calamus Estate Winery near Jordan, visitors and amateur astronomers can look deep into space and see interstellar bodies in significant detail at the Chronos Observatory. It looks much like a silo attached to the renovated barn.

The evening sky dramatically outlines Konzelmann Estate Winery on the shores of Lake Ontario in Niagara. Herbert Konzelmann chose this site for the winery in 1984 because of its meso-climate, which is similar to the Alsace region in France.

UPPER: After a morning rain the sun breaks through the clouds at Caroline Cellars, a family-owned and operated winery in Niagara-on-the-Lake.

LEFT: A vineyard gazebo overlooking Lake Ontario at Legends Estates Winery is an idyllic setting for a wedding. Many couples walk just a few steps away for photo ops between the rows of vines.

Sparkling glasses are at the ready in the Personalized Wine Experience Tasting Room at Thirty Bench Wine Makers in Beamsville.

Emerging leaves signal spring in the vineyards at Calamus Estate Winery in Jordan.

To cook in Niagara wine country is a chef's dream. The winemakers and farmers, your guides and pilots, set the course with their flavours and aromas and you follow along the path adding your two cents; a stir, a pinch, some heat and a splash. Boom! Delicious.

Michael Olson
Chef Professor, Niagara Culinary Institute

ABOVE: STURDY DOORS PROTECT THE ENTRANCE TO THE UNDERGROUND BARREL CELLAR AT CREEKSIDE ESTATE WINERY, ONE OF THE FIRST BUILT IN NIAGARA. SAUVIGNON BLANC VINES FLOURISH IN THE FIELDS BEYOND.

LEFT: A CHEF AT THE DECK AT CREEKSIDE OFFERS SEASONAL LUNCHES TO WEEKEND PATRONS THROUGHOUT THE SUMMER. CREEKSIDE ESTATE WINERY IS LOCATED IN JORDAN.

A well-protected William Roman of Rosewood Estates in Beamsville inspects the hive at the winery. Rosewood not only produces wine from its hand-harvested vineyards, but is also Niagara's first meadery or honey winery. Mead, the first fermented beverage enjoyed by modern mankind, dates back 10,000 years.

Daisies offer a feast for the eyes at Ravine Vineyard Estate Winery in St. Davids.

Grapes hang heavy on the vines, promising a good harvest.

upper: Louise Engel of Featherstone Estate Winery on the Niagara Escarpment prepares to let a predatory American kestrel falcon fly through the vineyard to deter nuisance birds from eating the grapes.

lower: After making its rounds, the kestrel will return to its controller.

ABOVE: EVEN THE AREA SURROUNDING THE GUEST BOOK IS STEEPED IN ATMOSPHERE AT MASTRONARDI ESTATE WINERY IN ESSEX COUNTY.

LEFT: A VISITOR ENJOYS A LITTLE SEPTEMBER SOLITUDE IN THE VINEYARDS AT ROSEWOOD ESTATES IN THE BEAMSVILLE BENCH.

A visit to Lake Erie North Shore and Pelee Island is a magical treat for the senses. Taste the passion that the vintners from 14 wineries produce … or the other offerings, abundant vegetables and herbs … from the rich soil in this, the southernmost part of Canada.

Chris Ryan
CEO, Tourism Windsor-Essex-Pelee Island

The morning sun breaks through the clouds at Pelee Island Winery in Kingsville.

ABOVE: SIP INTO SUMMER, AN EVENT HELD EACH JUNE AT COLIO ESTATE WINES IN HARROW, ESSEX COUNTY, FEATURES LOCAL VEGETABLES, BREAD, HERBS, JAZZ, AND, OF COURSE, WINES.

RIGHT: TIM REILLY, WINEMAKER AT COLIO, DRAWS SHIRAZ FROM A BARREL IN THE CELLAR TO CHECK ITS PROGRESS.

ABOVE: Wine tasters compare a "flight" or selection of various wines with an antipasto plate in the vineyard at Jackson-Triggs Niagara Estate Winery in Niagara-on-the-Lake.

RIGHT: Friends from Chicago on a Harley road trip stop at Sprucewood Shores Estate Winery at Harrow to enjoy a glass of Pinot Noir.

ABOVE: Toasting icewine marshmallows is one of the treats at Flat Rock Cellars in Jordan during Winterfest.

RIGHT: Founded in 1999 on a spectacular piece of the Niagara Escarpment known as the Jordan Bench, Flat Rock Cellars is perched on a gently rolling slope studded with vines. The winery building is a quirky, glass encased hexagon. Its crowning glory is a breathtaking view of the Niagara Peninsula and across Lake Ontario to Toronto.

The barrel cellar at Pillitteri Estates in Niagara-on-the-Lake features an impressive 42-foot monolithic concrete table with a terrazzo surface. Suspended above it are 23 stainless steel chairs, commissioned to symbolically tell the story of founders and proprietors Gary and Lena Pillitteri and their family, many of whom are involved in the operation.

I feel fortunate, as an Ontarian, to live in the heart of one of the world's most beautiful wine regions. Ontario wine country promises the chance to experience something truly magical and our cool climate allows us to produce wonderful wines that are a true reflection of our unique terroir. We have so much to be proud of and I encourage you to explore and discover the great treasures we have right here in our own backyard.

Hillary Dawson
President, Wine Council of Ontario

Signs of autumn indicate the grape harvest is approaching at Henry of Pelham Family Estate Winery. This family-run winery and founding member of the Vintner's Quality Alliance of Ontario (VQA) is located along the Short Hills Bench in St. Catharines. Its philosophy is that fine wines are grown, not made.

The distinctive hip-roofed barn of Hidden Bench Vineyards and Winery stands in a Pinot Noir vineyard along the Beamsville Bench.

A worker checks the vines on a hot October day at Hidden Bench.

ABOVE: It's time for a toast at the Wine Country Cooking School, which runs hands-on classes to explore the relationship between food and wine. The school, located at Strewn Winery in Niagara-on-the-Lake, offers one-day, two-day and five-day programs for recreational cooks.

LEFT: The bounty of the summer harvest is in all its glory at a fruit and vegetable stand along Lakeshore Drive in Niagara-on-the-Lake.

Guests sample the famous icewine at Inniskillin's recently renovated facility on the Niagara Parkway. The original post and beam ceiling was preserved from the site's old signature barn.

A wine tasting among the vines at Inniskillin is the highlight of the day for a group of friends from Virginia.

95

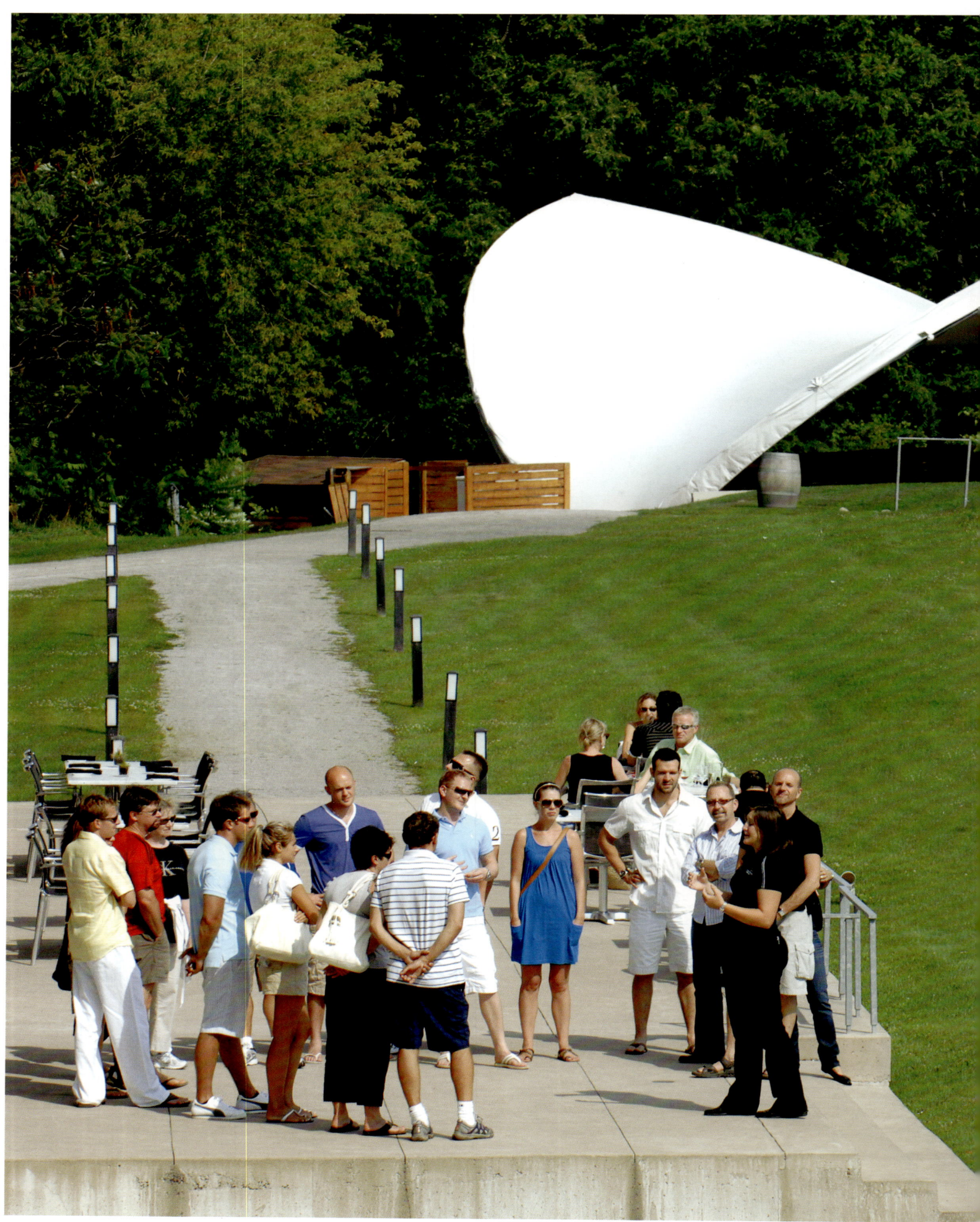

ABOVE: Hillebrand Blues at the Hillebrand Estates Winery in Niagara-on-the-Lake brings together Canadian musicians, fine wines, great local cuisine and lots of appreciative customers to enjoy them each August.

LEFT: A tour group hears about the winemaking process at Jackson-Triggs Niagara Estate Winery at Niagara-on-the-Lake.

UPPER: At Featherstone Estate Winery on the Twenty Mile Bench, sheep are brought to the rolling hills in mid-July to eat grape leaves, exposing the fruit to the sun.

LEFT: A small tractor is used to work the fields at Lailey Vineyard along the Niagara Parkway in Niagara-on-the-Lake.

upper: A "Vintage" way to explore Niagara's wineries is by riding the San Francisco-style trolley, pictured here at Jackson-Triggs Niagara Estate Winery. The trolley departs from the Vintage Hotel properties in Niagara-on-the-Lake.

lower: Grape pie and jams draw customers to a stand set up along Niagara Stone Road near Virgil.

Artist Vanessa Pandos works at Shattered, her studio and gallery in the Hillier region of Prince Edward County. She creates art from broken wine glasses.

ABOVE: After finishing a tour at Peller Estates Winery in Niagara-on-the-Lake, it's time for a break for carriage driver Chrissy and her trusty steed, Obie, from Sentineal Carriages.

RIGHT: The historic Claramount Inn & Spa in Picton is a great getaway while exploring Prince Edward County wine country. It is located in a gracious 1906 Colonial Revival home.

ABOVE: WHITE TABLECLOTHS AND BLACK TIES ARE NOT NECESSARY FOR THE ENJOYMENT OF A GLASS OF WINE IN THE AUTUMN SUNSHINE AT HUFF ESTATES WINERY IN PRINCE EDWARD COUNTY. VISITORS CAN STAY AT THE INN AT HUFF ESTATES AND TOUR THE OENO ART GALLERY.

RIGHT: HUFF ESTATES WINEMAKER FRÉDÉRIC PICARD SAMPLES THE HARVEST.

Taste, a festival held each September in Prince Edward County, gives visitors the opportunity to taste fine wines and treats such as the icewine truffles.

Visitors toast the regional cuisine, wineries, gifted chefs and jazz that make up the Taste Festival.

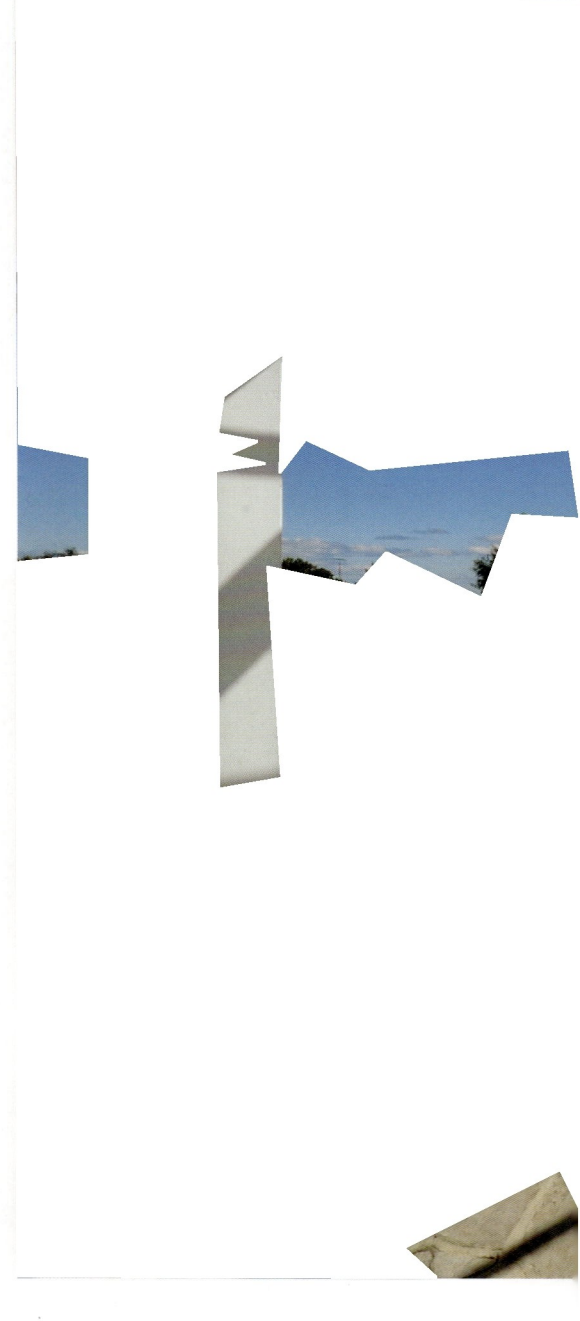

A sunny verandah overlooks vineyards at the entrance to Thirty Bench Wine Makers, a producer of premium wines from grapes grown exclusively on the estate vineyards in the Beamsville Bench appellation.

Ed Neuser, a proud pioneer of Prince Edward County's wine industry, overlooks his land at Waupoos Estates Winery on the shore of Lake Ontario.

Impressive pillars provide structural support in the barrel cellar at Peller Estates Winery in Niagara-on-the-Lake.

Although relatively youthful by comparison, Ontario's vineyards are ambitiously producing wines of award-winning world distinction. Growers and winemakers are using Ontario's unique terroir and combining technology with knowledge to craft memorable Ontario wines.

Debbie M. Zimmerman
CEO, Grape Growers of Ontario

ABOVE: THE WINE SENSORY GARDEN, THE FIRST OF ITS KIND IN NIAGARA, IS LOCATED AT REIF ESTATE WINERY. IT IS FILLED WITH PLANTS TO REMIND VISITORS OF THE COLOURS, FLAVOURS AND AROMAS OF THE WINE.

RIGHT: VISITORS ARRIVE IN STYLE FOR A TASTING AT PELLER ESTATES WINERY IN NIAGARA-ON-THE-LAKE.

ABOVE: Chef and author Tony de Luca, one of the architects of Niagara cuisine, still loves to spend time in the open kitchen at the Old Winery Restaurant in Niagara-on-the-Lake.

RIGHT: A five-course "deconstructed" vineyard dinner, which celebrates the sum total of the vine and its individual parts, is a special event at Stratus Vineyards in Niagara-on-the-Lake. Besides the wonderful cuisine and appropriate vintages, diners enjoy and a view of both the vineyard and courtyard.

Wine preferences are usually defined by our genetic heritage, but as we mature, so do our preferences. They are influenced by our familiarity with the wine, the pleasure experienced when a meal is accompanied by wine, but also by the cultural and socio-economic context in which the wine is consumed. Indeed, our research has shown that a great taste alone is not sufficient for a wine to sell; bottle label design and information, social pressure and word of mouth can affect the sensory experience when consumers taste and enjoy wine. Identifying the key motivations of consumer preferences for wine is critical to ensure market success of Ontario wines here and abroad. Our wines are among the best in the world, and they deserve all the attention we give them.

Dr. Isabelle Lesschaeve
Research Director, Consumer
Insights and Product Innovation
Vineland Research and Innovation Centre

VINES GIVE STRUCTURE TO THE GENTLY ROLLING HILLS OF THE MALIVOIRE WINE COMPANY ALONG THE BEAMSVILLE BENCH.

Late-autumn colours accessorize the contoured vineyards of Hidden Bench Vineyards and Winery along the Beamsville Bench.

Ontario wines are not only a reflection of the soil that produces the grapes, but of the people that have built an industry in the face of incredible odds. From the vines that have come to define the landscape to the wines that now reflect a way of life, Ontario wine country has become a part of the fabric of Canada's rich and diverse national identity.

Walter Sendzik, Founder, Vines Magazine
CEO, St. Catharines-Thorold Chamber of Commerce